WATCH
where
you walk

Lorimer Press, Davidson, North Carolina
Book Design, Leslie Rindoks
Printed in the United States

ISBN 978-0-9897885-6-4
Library of Congress Control Number: 2014959585

ACKNOWLEDGEMENTS

Thank you to the following publications where these poems appeared,
some in slightly different form.

Losses, *Yankee;* Fifth Voyage to Virginia, *England and Roanoke: A Collection
1584-1887;* Osteo, *Asheville Poetry Review;* Bodies, On the Chesapeake, Not
This Time, *Kakalak;* How One Woman Replaces Another, *Trapping Time
Between The Branches: Anthology;* The Only Thing I Fear, To Make Her Love
Me, Dirt, Mercury Mill, *The Only Thing I Fear Is A Cow and A Drunken Man;*
Widow, *St. Andrews Review;* Real Estate, *Poem;* Womanly, *Potato Eyes;* Eva's
Travels, *Spoon River Poetry Review;* Her Way of Talking, *Sunrust;* I Used To
Laugh, Three Women, *Tar River Poetry;* The Rider, *Spoon River Quarterly;*
Cedars, Seeing Carl Sandburg, *Christian Scientist Monitor;* Foolish Umbrella,
Living With A Man Who Loves John Wayne, *Davidson Miscellany;* His
Name Is Levi, *Arts Journal;* The Beast, *Greensboro Review;* Sweeping The
Clay, *Negative Capability;* Witch's Tale, *Nimrod;* Eve Level With Brown Peli-
cans, Of Mother and Father, *Shenandoah;* Coal Mine Town (titled In The
Time of John L. Lewis), *South Florida Review;* The Swimmer, *Briarpatch;*
Black and White, *Cardinal;* Where It Stands, *Wild Goose Review;* Horses,
Connecticut Writer; On The Steep Side, *Southern Appalachian Poetry: An An-
thology of Works by 37 Poets* and also in *New North Carolina Poets: The Eighties.*

My grateful thanks to The MacDowell Colony, Virginia Center for the
Arts, a grant from the North Carolina Arts Council, to all editors, and to
those remarkably gifted and generous women poets and fiction friends in
writer groups over the years.

WATCH
where
you walk

NEW &
SELECTED POEMS
by
Mary Kratt

Lorimer Press
Davidson, NC
2015

Also by Mary Kratt

POETRY
Small Potatoes
Valley
The Only Thing I Fear Is a Cow and a Drunken Man
On The Steep Side
Spirit Going Barefoot

NON-FICTION
Charlotte, North Carolina: A Brief History
A Bird in the House: The Story of Wing Haven Garden
New South Women: Twentieth Century Women of Charlotte, North Carolina
Edward M. O'Herron, Jr.: An Extraordinary Life
Remembering Charlotte: Postcards from a New South City, 1905-1950 (with Mary Boyer)
The Imaginative Spirit: Literary Heritage of Charlotte and Mecklenburg County
Legacy: The Myers Park Story (with Thomas W. Hanchett)
A Little Charlotte Scrapbook
Charlotte: Spirit of the New South
Marney
My Dear Miss Eva
Southern Is…

CONTENTS

CONTENTS, *continued*

On The Thistle Path

for others who walk the thistle path

WATCH WHERE YOU WALK

Thistles.
      Savor the purple blooms,
the prickly contrast.

      Barbed,
beautiful in bloom
      they crowd the green pasture
beyond the window
      and
far in the distance,
      our hilly meadow.

         Bring your hoe.

OUT OF BACK CREEK

Tales of mavericks, mayhem
and heroines in a mostly competent clan –
Mother is one,
a country preacher's daughter, black eyes
and curly hair, not quite five feet
and lively. Lord yes, she talked her way
to teaching out of Back Creek, Long Creek,
Pisgah, Mount Ulla, and a town
called Prosperity.
In childhood on long Sabbath afternoons
with no comics, cards, or radio,
her brothers wheeled Mother up and down
the center aisle in the coffin cart,
all for fun. Fun was foremost

although she was Martha who named
me Mary. She would not teach me to mop,
You'll learn soon enough.
At the table, I heard kinfolks' tales
while she toiled hot in the kitchen. Martha,
who sang, cooked, and storied,
recalling her mother
with hands deep in dishwater
saying, *Sing, child, sing.*
You can't think dark thoughts
while you're singing.

THE SWIMMER

Polio caught her as a child in the parsonage,
1916, far from town. Grandpa, the preacher,
took off his belt, put it round her waist
and held her up in the pond to paddle, to swim,
to kick her feet like the city doctor said.
And in high school near the giant Loray Mill
was that indoor pool, the county marvel
where she swam.

Decades later in the doctor's office,
a nurse asked: *Surgery? Hospitalizations?*
Mother answered, *Two births, two miscarriages*
despite the long scar on her heel and the twisted walk.
But what about polio? I whispered. *Hush*, she said.

MARTHA, WHO NAMED ME MARY

determined
not to take on
that tether,
her apron worn
serving brothers seven
and Father,
and live-in guest,
the missionary's son
whom she detested.
Years
he sat,
his feet under
under their oak table
while she bustled
back
and forth serving
food her mother
cooked – baskets
of biscuits,
cauldrons of mush,
salvers of fried chicken
plucked
from the fowl yard,
blackberry pies
from prickle canes
found
in a chiggery field.

She was
the daughter Martha,
servant, scrubber.
I am her daughter
Mary.
Do you remember
that long-ago Martha?
She complained to Jesus
of sister Mary,
who sat listening.
She's not
helping!
He did not mind.

LATIN ENDINGS

After lunch, Father slept.
Time was a hammock he fell into
while Mother made berry tarts,
Grandmother rocked and told tales
to anybody who'd listen,
while little brother slept
and out back I made mud pies.
Early mornings, 1970s, Mother stood
in her slippers, the pink robe
she'd not throw away, a woman
who collected rocks from Walden, Rio
and Rome, who still remembered
Latin endings. She told stories – true, she said –
but stretched, we knew. And Father
made a list each morning.
In January with seed catalogs,
his mental ground ready, weather was his eye.
There were few earth places
he could not make do. I keep the memory,
how we three buried their son, my brother.
What could be hard after those long nights?

OSTEO

Like a perpetual oriental,
she bows
without intending.
As though the old creator,
that odd puppeteer,
finally
pulled her string,
she leans and cannot rise.
Year by year,
she tightens,
angles,
her straight days
behind her.
She is life's question mark
although all week long
she gave us
admonitions like peppermints.

YES

Everywhere, like daylily blooms,
        some are dying,
        like the man across the street,
whose first words when I moved in,
        Your shrubs, take them out!
                and now he's taken.

        Nancy, last week starting chemo, says,
My hair will fall out by Friday. She's picked
                a wig.

        In the market at my elbow
wait people I rarely notice because
        after cancer, divorce, or both,
                they look like anybody.

Yet everywhere they are living:
        Mother, 98, follows Tiger Woods
and the Cubs, mocks women at her table, their strange
        quirks and talk. She measures a book
by its heft on her chest for bed reading,
        checking the last page first so she won't
                waste time on desperate endings.

Meanwhile in my yard, each daylily bloom lifts
        its only day,
        raising its *yes* to the sun.

FIELD TRIP FROM ASSISTED LIVING

At the door of Mother's room,
the activities director asks,
Miz Norton,
moving to Mother's bed,
Would you like to go with us
on the mystery ride?
Quickly, Mother answers,
Honey, I AM on a mystery ride.

SOMEBODY ELSE'S

I sewed labels on, I'm sure.
Her name
and the number of her room, so
after laundry her clothes could
find their way
maybe not directly,
but finally back to her
in assisted living.
But someone else's slacks came back
and since they did not fit,
Mother with her scissors slashed
the waist to fix it,
sliced it like a steak, a sheet.
They were fixed all right.

AFTER MONTHS OF SILENCE

Some days, the nurses told me,
Mother preached in the hall,
quoted Bible verses, Shakespeare,
hymns, or finished the devout
social worker's prayers.
She even lectured
on invertebrate animals,
although her career
was Latin and high school English.
But for months, when I come,

                Silence.

Again, I lean close,
I've been to the farm stand
to buy tomatoes
like Dad used to grow.
Remember?

                Silence.

I'm going home now
to fix tomato sandwiches

                Silence.

Good bread. Bacon.
Lettuce. Mayonnaise.
And tomatoes.

Here's one,
the tomato rolls red
in her hands, hot and ripe as July.

Tomato sandwiches,
she says clearly. *But we*
didn't have bacon.

NOT THIS TIME

Before I left town
I said goodbye,
kissed her and at the door,
stood and gazed as she lay
slack in bed, 99 and stranded
on the rugged beach of age.
This is it, I thought.
It's time, the nurse had said.
Each day away,
each phone call might
have been the one. But
when I returned, she
sat dressed in the hall.
You're back, she said
in her purple hat.

You're back, I said
taking off my coat,
What have you been doing?
I asked.

She answered firmly,
Going here and there
with my mother.
We had lots to do.

YOU WOULD

Since she cannot see
or hear, Mother does not
know me, or might not even if
she could. She wanders mists
beyond her bed, far from me.
With her thin, cool hands in mine,
she travels hillsides –
Switzerland. Granada. Rome.

But this time
she mistakes me for the nurse or aide
or kind Cindy from the church.
What she picks to tell them
is not about her son, the favorite, who died,
not fishing with my father,
or singing with her mother,
not one fond wisp of song or poem.
She offers instead
whisper soft,
You would like my daughter.

WAITING ON SALVATION

Always expecting
it would come,
but not so late as this,
hours waiting
with Mother's bags labeled –
clothes, bedding, shoes,
a gaudy, gilded dresser
leftover at the nursing home,
surfaces scarred
by wanton spills.
The dispatcher says,
I'm four stops away
from pickup,
this last deliverance
into other grateful arms.

THE KNIFE
After her death

They got to talking about the past,
that near country never far,
the time cousin Chris visited Mother,
how in the middle of her story
she limped to her dresser
in that last small room of her life,
drew from a drawer of underwear and purple scarves
way at the back, the butcher knife, large
and old, its blade notched with frantic teeth irregular
like a small scarred sword at ready,
an object she was not, of course, supposed to have,
in her nineties in assisted living.

Then she described the doctor's phone call
thirty years before, an answer at last
to the mystery of why her son's legs
slowed and dragged,
that he had ALS, the creeping horror
that killed Lou Gerhig by inches,
until only his eyes and mind
remained alive. She told Chris how she hung up
the phone and snatched her biggest knife
from the kitchen drawer, ran to the woods out back
and there attacked the giant oak, her rage so huge
and she so small, a fury, again again again.

As he tells it, I remember –
long after her son's slow death at 38 and later hers,
I found the knife and tossed it in the trash, without a clue
to what it was or why.

HONOR

> *your father*
> *and mother,*

it says,
that commandment
of old,
the fourth of ten,
and I do
agree,
as I should,
mostly.

      I did
honor them
but not
why
the ancient law
demands,
promises,

> *that your days*
> *may be long*
> *upon the land*
> *the Lord*
> *your God*
> *gives you.*

      No.
I, who bear
their
fierce
genes
of longevity,
after honoring
through their nineties,
discover
love,
the far better reason.

FAR COUNTRY

On the thistle path
            no one is singing
                        or tells
where we are headed.

Neither stones
            nor wild grasses
                                    say
how far we are to go.

The Edge

FOUR TOMBSTONES

Lorenzo Hunter had three wives,
three lives for the asking.
Over Ann's grave
he rooted two twigs,
English boxwoods
from their farmhouse yard.
She was the first.

Two feet west
he buried Martha
who lies in graveyard sun,
lonesome as empty Sundays.
She was the second.

In the new cemetery across the road
Lorenzo lies by his last wife, Dovey,
a widow from up the county.
No children, but she gave more.
She was the third.

Kinfolk say
he left Ann's land to Martha's children —
old Lorenzo lying across the road
with Dovey.

HOW ONE WOMAN REPLACES ANOTHER
IS THE OLDEST STORY

One night the darkness
climbs the window
differently.
There is no name for this,
but something closed.

When he left,
he opened every window
and door, left
every light on,
curtains flying.
It does no good
to buy a new dress.
He has gone
where there is no key
for you,
no door.

THREE WOMEN

Night is a net drawing toward us
from the silent lake,
our talk hauls it up the darkening mountain
onto the porch
where we stay gathered,
our chairs curled together
until we are the only world visible,
but for the absent woman,
the one we speak of,
the friend who's run away
with her lover to Florida.
We thought we knew her.
The details – how and possible
whens – rise into oak leaves
and shagbark hickory
like smoke,
like resonant steam,
and one by one we sit in the dark,
emptied of talk, idle
as gloves on a dressing table,
our thoughts like moths circling.

ACROSS THE ROOM

The furry, brown buffalo head above the bar
stares down as we eat our lasagna.
And at a nearby table, I stare at a man's back,
his jacket and curly hair.
He was my first date, a tall city boy
whose father drove him out in the county
to bring me to the dance. Yesterday
I passed the small white house in woods
on that country road,
the door he knocked on, his father waiting
in the green car, motor running.
I was so grateful
he came far to get me,
I want to cross the room
to tell my sudden thanks,
but even the buffalo staring down,
says no.

HOW TO ATTRACT AN OLDER MAN

Wear
    A perky straw
Be younger
    Smile and listen
Be willing
    Curb strong opinions
Laugh at his jokes
    Tell yours
Laugh at yourself
    Not at him
Don't say
    You snore
He will reply
    You do, too
Dress for yourself
    Glad in your own skin

AT THE BRITISH MUSEUM

Old Kingdom Egyptians
had a way out
and here I stand
still as a sphinx
by their false doors
carved in stone,
an exit
to let dead spirits travel,
offerings left
before priests sealed
the passage forever,
that last slant of light waning.
And this boat for travels,
as if placing it there made it true.
This magic they knew.
On solid stone
an etched door
could open and close
if they thought so.
A boat in a sealed room
could weather any sea.

TEMPS PERDU
At the Musée Carnavalet, Paris

Is there no end, no beginning –
this story of Paris, *l'histoire?*
Fragments from the past
in this ancient mansion: stones
from the Bastille, the single brass bed
where Proust wrote, a ballroom elegante,
an entire jeweler's shop art nouveau
from buildings long since lost,
a Neolithic dugout canoe
and famous Madame de Sévigné,
her portrait as she lived here writing
witty letters which friends copied
and sent around, three centuries ago.
The guide in blue talks softly, dwarfed
by *Louis Quatorze* , high on a pedestal, regal
and bewigged. As long as I smile
when I ask halting questions in French,
natives seem far kinder
than their history of tribes, wars, intrigue,
except for pickpockets
in the guise of giggling young girls. I
am disarmed even without my stolen wallet –
how all things here are more than old, like
blood and beauty, ever new.

SPIRITS

Here in New England
above my head
the lid of the porch
is painted blue,
that spirit-wary hue
of New Orleans, Natchez,
Savannah, Charleston,
whose antique porch ceilings
sometimes wear
this otherworldly skrim
paler than birdshell.

You may not notice
(among all-white walls
and window trim),
this uncanny primer,
a primitive porch-roof skin.

Someone has seen,
or felt what's loose,
provided a charm
overhead to warn
off malevolent spirits.
A visible incantation.
Walk under it
like a phantom
among phantoms.

ALMOST THERE

In the scratchy backseat
of the new blue Studebaker,
we curl in the dark,
sleep our way down the mountain
hurtling from Allegheny to Tidewater
with Father up front aiming headlights
toward the home place on the water.

As my brother and I drift in and out of dreams,
our open car windows sift smells of night:
mossy forest, smoky mountain valleys,
dust and manure of foothill pastures. Down
and down we ride, as blinking
village lights glide by,
and the road levels out past Hopewell
to the hot, wet dark of Bottoms Bridge.

At old battlegrounds,
our lights catch markers
and if we're awake, Father tells us again
how his grandfather bled there
and died from a musket ball.
Onto the tire-singing metal
of the long drawbridges,
we cross the Pamunkey,
the Mattaponi, and he makes us repeat
those river names.

And when forever has come and gone,
the stench of the paper mill
draws us close at last
to the tall house by the water.
At dawn we drive in,
find aunts fixing biscuits
and fried fish for breakfast.
They point us to the plump ripe figs
by the well house and blue crabs
that skitter into their black, bay-bottom holes
dark now as our mountain house
we left at midnight.

That early morning in the tidewater yard
my brother and I can't know
he will die young
as we gather figs the color of bruises
handful by sticky handful.

ON THE CHESAPEAKE

The wind is from the south
and boats turn into it.
Swallows with their peach bellies
and chittery calls,
sail over the wet black dog
who noses his last route around.

This is that time toward evening
when all the boats change;
in our deep cove, they rise
with light, as though Turner
or some other master
saw and taught them shining.

The light holds.
The people below decks,
how can they miss this?
All photographs are photographs of light.
Sensing daylight go, does a woman murmur,
What was that just now? as though something
huge and delicate passed by.

FAREWELL MY WATERMAN FATHER

Toss one white funeral rose
on the outgoing tide. All
I can do is gaze
as it drifts
past his weathered dock,
floats and bobs
in the fading Chesapeake light,
passes the buoy,
the osprey nest,
and the forested cove –
one rose, diminishing white.

IF I TAKE MY EYES AWAY

In grey blue feathers
the heron,
stately
on green water,
wades this way
and that,
then waits in shallows,
spears something shiny,
an awkward gulp,
no ripples.

If I take my eyes away,
then look back,
he is not there. But
he is there
like this ache for you
who will no longer gaze
at sails, buoys, the dock
or search whitecaps
warning of rough weather.

WHERE IT STANDS

There,

      that one tree

            anchors the whole island

                  with its sturdy slant.

Were it not exactly

      where it stands

            on the green slope

                  across the water,

would not the island,

      the whole precarious world,

            slide into the sea?

LOST RIVER

By the old bridge
      looking south toward the meadow,
you stand where this stream vanishes
      like smoke in the wind,
            like beauty we did not know we had
until it goes.

On our map, this river wanders,
      then loses itself
until an inch south
      its dark line flows again
            past the town of Lost River,

disappearing among grasses,
      like the day you came home
with the doctor's word for your disease,
            and our lives plunged underground.

Although the land wears green
      and cows collect in the far trees' shade,
beneath us the river courses silent, patient.
            All day, all night, we know it's there.

THE EX-SMOKER

This man
lying here beside me
needs a cigarette
even in his sleep.
He's dreaming an airplane
and he's the only passenger,
smokes at will
above L.A., Grand Canyon,
O'Hare, making smoke rings
above Ghost Ranch,
over Mt. St. Helens,
Hawaii's volcanoes.

He dreams the finest restaurant
and he's smoking in the best seat,
the corner with a view.
The head waiter knows him.
On every table, an ashtray
even two, each one's his
and yes sir someone waits
to empty them.

Happy, restless sleeper,
he's both Bogart and Bacall.

LIVING WITH A MAN WHO LOVES JOHN WAYNE

When you marry, there are things
you can't know, like whether he'll be bald,
remember birthdays, or
merely look at other women.

You never know what will ask the most,
like thirty years of John Wayne movies,
how nothing else goes on in the world
when Duke is riding, even when
you know what the sheriff will say
and how many swigs it takes
for Rooster Cogburn to get True Grit.

I never knew it would be John Wayne,
born Marion Morrison of Iowa,
who would gallop our empty evenings,
paunch one night, tenderfoot the next,
all his battles over by bedtime,
saint of the audible screen,
immortal mortal cowboy who loved tequila,
wanted his true-life tombstone to read
He was ugly. He was strong.

ALWAYS

Like the long journey
of our marriage, this Carolina road
is scarred and sacred.
Look, the same ceramic boy in red
fishes his pond always
beside this road we've traveled twenty years.
I notice how
a cotton field flips to tractor factory,
latticed barns yield
to a trailer park, and placid cows gathered
for milking melt
into equestrian houses with paddocks
and endless fences.

Like marriage, it's a two lane road –
yesterday winter, today spring
as the stranded dogwoods
in a timbered forest bloom white
against the dark of winter bark,
a promise sure as the old river
that flows around its stubble islands.
We cross the rocky Haw, a river
never navigable except at floodtide.
Beyond is the circle of oaks
where the old man waved
from his porch chair each time we passed.
He was always there. The house is gone.
He's gone too,
still we wave.

OXYGEN

Breathing in
breathing out
          hums the machine in the next room
sends life invisible
through the thin clear hose
          its sound like a hot air balloon
floating pulsing low overhead.

While eggs fry at breakfast
the machine's rhythms echo
a heavy hum, into bedrooms and
          beside children's pictures –
grandson with his violin, two more
on a hike with walking sticks
stopped for a moment smiling and there
the photograph of our infant granddaughter
          in her mother's arms.

Those years you smoked one cigarette
          even while you lit another,
now the heavy shadow we knew waited –
your breath's tether
          a fifty-foot transparent tube
trails you like a willing servant
throughout the house
          and down the long white hall.

These Woods

ANYTHING CAN EMERGE AT THE EDGE OF THESE WOODS

A unicorn on giraffe's legs
a rolling tire with a boy inside
cockatoos chased by bluebirds
your neighbor in a bikini
and that wolf, remember
always waiting in shadows?

From these pines and moist undergrowth
love could rise – trouble or tenderness
anything at all, so watch as if
you are a forest ranger or lighthouse keeper
a bordello madam searching
far and near for a bagel with a red sail unfurled
and no one steering toward a hunter's moon.

LOSSES

Years after the hurricane,
the woods still whisper.
The last great trunks lean bare as matches
from that night of wind.
Bark hangs like snakeskins.

In these dead, blunt watchtowers,
woodpeckers carve high caves. They wait
as I, surviving loss,
find at last a way to use it.
Since that long night, nothing is the same.

How strong it still is,
this presence of absence.
Where shadows were, now sun,
where moss, brambled roses
and viney young dogwoods.
The earth knows how to recover.
She does not say this is bad,
this is good, this is mine.

After a week of rain,
a heavy crash wakes me —
another great tree has fallen,
pocked and stripped and rotting,
where mice, ants, grubs will shelter
and raccoons at night
will peel things delicious
with their small, fastidious hands.

WAITING

for something grand
like romance
an infant's birth
a startle voice
a slice of freedom
or perhaps
a turtle sunning
on the mossy foot log
a kingfisher
with his raspy far-off call
his plummet into the pond
or deer beyond the audible curtain
of cicadas.

We look for grandeur
for beauty long and long
but sometimes
it is only a beetle
and here is one   shiny black
long as my thumb
unhurried   determined
shifting leaves as he goes
and a slight breeze.
Don't forget that.

TRESTLE TRAIL

> To hike and find
the trail, friends gather each October,
lace boots one yellow morning and climb
through rhododendron shade, scarlet oaks,
rosy sourwoods, the steep red dirt path
reamed with ruts and rocks, and galax,
that calm green heart. Stop here,
one says, and sits breathless on a log,
its bark clawed clean.

> But this year, no one could
climb that high trail where a century ago,
loggers cleared the forest. Mature again,
the woods wait in stippled light.
With Sue's racing heart, Ann's bad knee,
we at last are tamed,
and stroll to a round pool, earth's water eye
of golden blaze, silence,
and open sky. No one says how loss
is found even if we look away,
how loss can carry something new or fine.
Wind scuds one leaf, a valiant Viking bark
across the water.

PATCH

On the rug's warm
patch where sun
peers in, here is
the place to sit. To
slumber. To remind me
of my friend's cousins
from England,
who that chill
April afternoon lay
in bathing suits
on the one far
corner of her yard
against woods.
The corner where
afternoon sun kept shining.
The corner where
her dog always peed.

YOU SAW IT TOO

Expecting no more
than the usual grace of morning
on tall hemlocks and oaks,
we look from the porch
as sun crests the mountain,
firing spider webs – hundreds –
like a vast luminous cape.

If we stand just right,
silver gleams for an instant.
A final October orb
weaves the black bark of the forest,
and in a breath and shifting light,
it goes. But you saw it too
in a whisker of time,
brief as life, as love,
as rare.

PULLING UP STAKES

Not me, not me
though I considered it.
There across our pond
someone pulled up those offending
red-flagged swords of wood announcing
Lot 81, Lot 82 right at our water's edge.

Winter trees wait bare as facts
to witness raw stakes that suddenly
proclaim the line we always knew was there.
Sunday morning crows argue
Methodist bells across the hill. Shivering
beech leaves whisper, but don't tell
who marked the land last week or who tossed
stakes aside like errant saplings. A half century

ago, Father bought this land.
Here is the pond he dug and stocked and fished
and there, the boundary seen or unseen
beyond this calm. Step over it. The hillside
looks like ours. But seeing now
the red-flagged plan for woods that edge our water
is like the shadow of a turkey vulture, casual
as clouds above miles of woods and fields scanning

quarry. I swivel on my sitting stump
to watch the woods we own - a view more comforting –
sweet water springs, green field, pastures, ravine
of scrub pine, oak and berries. Turtles sunning.
What farmer once owned it all? Perhaps he paced off
these twenty acres to buy a child's surgery,
a cow or yellow tractor, and sighed
the day he signed the deed.

TREES OF THE SOUTHERN FOREST

Scarlet oak and loblolly pine,
water oak and willow –
name labels along the path,
this last place Father and I strolled
before he walked
into the wide cave of the hospital.

Pin oak, post oak, white oak.
He was a fisherman, teacher, principal,
and after the Great Depression,
a newspaperman. Around our hilly yard
hemlock, white pine, pussy willow,
the red stalks of rhubarb, silky corn.
And stalwart hives of bees.

Black gum, sweet gum, sourwood.
In the retirement home, his tomatoes
climbed stakes by his window
while he interviewed his neighbors,
drove widows to the airport, told stories of his city
and trees to educate the Yankees, he said.

Tulip poplar, hickory, beech.
In the years since he died,
I walk the woods path
and find his fading labels
nailed to tree bark along this lane
in his last, quiet classroom.

Black jack oak, cedar, shortleaf pine.
When the names split with tree growth,
 I hammer them back
to stretch our leafy conversation. I walk slow
as he did toward the last, avoid the hill.
Dogwood, walnut, sassafras.
Scarlet oak. Loblolly pine.

NIGHT

Blue-dark night falls on the mountain
severing earth and sky,
day's heaven of light yielding
to star and beacon in the valley.
All mountains become
one black monolith of earth –
Monadnock, Mitchell, Ararat and Sinai –
where God hides. Night
is to watch, to lie down with,
sheltering fear in its closet,
sorrows without names.

On the porch where light is last to go,
we write our lives – pages to years.
For the book of handmade paper,
its soft leather cover, what life, what word
is beautiful enough? What life isn't?
A star comes down to the edge of the mountain,
how much does it know?

from

On The Steep Side

ON THE STEEP SIDE

Everything rolled down in West Virginia.

Potatoes, dug in the garden, tumbled
to the backdoor. Houses clung
to inclines like cicada shells to tree bark.
Molasses vats filled deeper at one end
cooked late by torchlight near the barn.
And our picnic watermelon, toppling from the car,
rolled like a cannonball to the lake,
split, floated like two pink islands.

Climbing to Mount Hope
one curve, walled with coal,
rose like a torn shoulder of that dark
nether giant who held our lives;
and everywhere men's faces blackened with dust,
lanterned miner's hats with the third eye.

Downhill to the mine's wind tunnel
we walked railroad ties on Sunday afternoons,
dug sassafras roots coming home.
We owned the land's crust for house, rhubarb,
potatoes. Underneath
belonged to the mine. Blasts jiggled
cups in the kitchen.

From Grand View I got the sense
that level was for common people.
When we moved down
to lowland Carolina where some thought
humps were hills and hills were mountains,
the steep eye stayed mine
and saved me from a level life.

WORDS FROM A RUSSIAN WITCH'S TALE:
THE MORNING IS WISER THAN THE EVENING

The witch, Baba Yaga, in her house held up by hen's legs,
lived at the corner of my steep street.
Fearing she would knock at my door, I hid and dreamed
book countries in the corner of the wide-oak floor,

palaces beyond glass mountains of my coal mine town.
I was the least, the plainest peasant daughter
hoping for the gift her father brings. An apple
on a magic dish. Roll it around until the plate is a window

to any land I wish. Mine is not a tale told lightly.
the little wooden doll I kept in my pocket,
whose eyes burned like embers, spoke to me at night
of alchemy and all things possible.

COAL MINE TOWN

When we threw ripe tomatoes
at Patty Morrison's window,
we'd never heard of caste or class.
Our fathers were white collar,
hers came home black all over
sooty, carrying a lunchbox,
still wearing his miner's helmet
with its one brass eye.
We never wondered
how the Morrisons managed
to move up from Coal Town
to our middle-class hill.
I forget street names
and all our little secrets,
but what comes back is the splat
against glass and Patty's cheeks, red
as tomatoes.

SEEING CARL SANDBURG

It was dark when we found it.
White, just somebody's house,
that night my parents
drove crooked roads
to sit in a room
with one swinging overhead light
and hear the visitor,
a shirt-sleeved, green-visored poet
who played a guitar. We
were West Virginia. He
was Chicago, his hair cream-bright.
My first guitar, first poet.
He spoke words plain as whole notes
and later down the mountain
we carried them.

SWEEPING THE CLAY

Imagine children sweeping
clay's red floor clean of pine.
I play mother
trying certainty each morning
as I sweep,
redraw transparent borders, walls
for the husband I do not know.
After I bathe, he will walk
through the door.
Our door, the arm of a scarlet oak.

Patiently I wait for my cousin
coming to play sister, guest, child,
sometimes doing as she is told
in this fresh air future.
We mind the wet mud stove
made by our red clay fingers,
shaped to a little door,
holding cakes of childhood,
scones small as breasts rising.

Try to see us always knowing
how clay is free as pine,
the only thing no one else wants.

The ground I swept
like the bed I slept on
yielded dreams we needed.
Dirt was the nearest thing we owned,
giving ice spears in winter,
and summer,
those cracks of clay deep
enough to lose our lives down.

LISTEN TO LEVI

The old dog hunts dream woods,
    asleep in the kitchen,
he quivers on blue linoleum –
    his rabbit, lost down a burrow
over the high, green hill.

    When sirens go by,
Levi moans a long sound
    no one knew was in him.
It is in us all,
    the old cry siding up with sorrow,
the sound of it not far off.

Night
    and the back door slams.
I take down the dog leash
    to go walking.
On the meadow path
    evening light closes around us.
The world stands back
    at the edge.
Woods don't breathe
    as long as
we range the high grass field
    where everything is ours.
We are everything's!
    Downhill,
earth is again the place we know.

BLACK AND WHITE

The preacher who urges risk taking
isn't with me the day
I walk the empty hall
to the art center darkroom,
find the black man
timing his prints in the developing tray.
I am a white woman who thinks she has
much to lose, who was warned
so early she cannot remember.
And he is very tall there tilting trays
moving a picture back and forth in liquid.

.

I am a moment without defenses
like a woman unpinning her hair.
By the dim safelight I begin,
hoping it is safe to share
this close, shadowy room,
alone in the urban building,
conjuring images lured outside
into cameras, our curious handheld eye.

Like an answer,
the old woman's face slowly rises
from chemical paper,
her face looking all possible kindness,
her shapeless dress,
armchair in front of a stove.
The calendar on her wall finally reads August.

All these buoyant pictures,
lines of noses, hands, leaves, the Hotpoint
stove behind his grandmother,
she in the room with us floating,
her eyes.

HORSES

Each morning blew them
from the barn as though light called
their motion together
to the pasture's far corner, where
honeysuckle reached for their muscles, skin,
like the abundant pleasure of God.
I would stand at the fence among cedars
and survey my neighbor's pasture,
watch his horses grazing and playful,
and always the chestnut, the leader, and
how the mare followed. The first time they saw me
I stood at the line of my field and theirs,
cedars hiding the fence stretched between.
I pretended I was a cedar, so straight,
but they knew, running back and forth, nervous,
watching. I was an eye among vines.
I stayed. They settled, grazed warily
not far from my stillness.
And then they knew me.

Mornings I came to watch silence
and motion. I stood among leaves
admiring the black and the chestnut,
his huge sex dangling like a dark accordion,
and I saw childhood horses far in the field,
that coupling we cousins never spoke of
though we saw how they finished, went on grazing.

The horses are gone
in a van to Montana, along with the rooster's
early announcements, gone with the white dog
who came by at breakfast.

I shall not miss the sear
of the boy's go-cart motor.
But the horses, I look for them
among cedars, their running up from the barn
as I measure storm damage
before traffic's low hum begins in the distance
or evenings when the boy comes out, the small whip
he snaps crack, crack, a sound like no other
and they hurry toward him. He turns them running
at last to the barn.

It is evening without the horses.
Montana's deep sky, the great winding river,
hills like my life stretched out waiting,
not these close woods. And I see horses.
The chestnut looks up for a moment, goes on grazing.

THE BEAST

In John Gardner's tree
a beast climbed,
merely ceramic,
fixed in winter's daylight,
New England dark,
fanged and wild-eyed
into summer, a medieval joke
of a precocious child.

Lying beside you tonight
at the edge of woods,
far from New England,
far from Grendel,
we hear a rasping howl,
and struggle from sleep
as again it rises

like the dream you always dreamed
returning, the bad witch
who called your name, or
the sound of something you knew
out there roaming. Not the snake

we watched glide
across the roof at dusk. You thought
wind had ripped the top shingles,
but the black hump oozed
on. High as elms, it followed
the long roof length, then slid
down the downspout, careful, careful
like a strange, beautiful thing,

but now, this sound, wild
like a torn roar,
you hear it too,
and it's not all right,
the last beast loose
within me, waiting
close as night.

TO GUARD THE HOUSE

While they go to the funeral,
we stay with the house
not that it would escape without us.
We answer the phone,
show those who'd take advantage of death
we are here.
The house isn't abandoned.
I see nothing I would steal
if I preyed on survivors.
Biscuits wrapped in saran.
Pies. Pound cakes. Ham.
A stack of books on miracle healing.
None of the remedies worked.

Someone calls for her.
She's not here,
but the telephone voice insists,
Give her a message. How do I say
no message will get through.

Downstairs we talk in matching chairs
flanking the fireplace,
facing the door and all furies
in a cave of continuous green
walls, curtains, velvet chairs,
plush with our murmur of kin
who came to sit for solace, talk family,
Wasn't she pretty? who resembles who,
and *What will he do without her?*
We chat trips and funeral plots. We talk rain
and new folks on down the road.
Like mild lions we guard this house
whose worst thief has already come.

EYE LEVEL WITH BROWN PELICANS

A stretch of beach
and tall, pink condos
banded by white balconies.
Each day
in front of our hotel
the boy plants umbrellas
like painted pine trees –
a perfect, tiny line of yellow,
red, and blue, five each,
two chairs apiece, and
up the beach a trailer
park's bright laundry flies
and supper smells
and shouts arise with every
body's music while
brown pelicans soar over,
following their leader.
Like us, they're flying
toward extinction.
From my hotel we're eye to eye,
above calypso bands
that sway in heat
to steel drums' beat
down by the pool.
One elderly woman
alone on a back staircase
breaks into a dance step.
If this is what God sees
how he must love us each
for such inept dimension,
color, stubbornness
against a tide, the land,
and this small stretch of beach.

Valley
&
Spirit Going Barefoot

CATCHING THE MORNING TRAIN
Boyce and Eva, 1898

Eva married him.
So early, not too late
to catch the train
at 9 a.m. on Groundhog Day
and when they finally
climbed aboard,
he stowed his coat,
her trunk and carpetbag,
and they sat down shy
at last alone.
He'd hardly
held Eva's hand until that morning
when the sideburned preacher
married them at seven
by the parlor fireplace
at Kerr's Creek. Her parents
and sisters smiled, then
brothers chased them out
with a lilting wedding march played
on harmonicas. Snow swept
the horse and carriage hitched and ready,
waiting for the couple
to catch the train from Lexington
to a life that rose before them
like House Mountain,
a life
they could never imagine.

EVA'S TRAVELS

She was a packed suitcase,
a stamped letter, a hitchhiker
with both thumbs out.
Widowed young, she became
that extra relative in all our lives
moving from son to daughter to son.
She never could, never would learn to drive.
Her hat and purse lay on the sideboard and she'd go
where anybody was headed.
In the days of her own house,
her own sink and kitchen window,
she had looked beyond chicken-plucking,
appleskins, sauce, and jam,
pecks and bushels in from the yard,
a wall of fruit jars waiting on winter,
and every day, nine plates
set on the table behind her.
Out that window rose one blue mountain
each day she climbed with her eyes.

WOMANLY

When she put on the corset,
Grandmother entered its circle
as a diva embraces the hall

but with no applause,
wrapped it round her,
long peach Venetian shade

threaded with stays, strung with strings.
She gathered her breasts
to enclose them,

two pendulous tongues,
breasts
like they had been pressed.

I am the silent child
who helped lace
the corset this ladder

hooks zigzagging
tie at the top a long white string

fixing a hardness
not hers.
She smiled at me there in the mirror.
I, just beginning.

REAL ESTATE

Grandmother loved houses, but
we never went in. We drove
close enough for possibilities
every Sunday
as we rode from town,
searched for that mountain farm
we would always buy.
All those valleys,
we drove through slowly,
then paused, our car motor running,
Mother and Father in front, all of us
gazing just beyond our lives.
Out the window I bought a barn,
and saw myself, a cow's soft
teat in my hand, squirt a long thread
of milk to a cat named Sam.

Many a road led nowhere or wrong
and, as it got thinner and deeper rutted,
Grandmother got out of the car
in her chin-length veil, feathered hat, stood
in her long black coat and gloves
like a dark antique while son-in-law
see-sawed the Studebaker back and forth
so close to the edge turning around.
Her life had been scary enough,
thank you.

In the car riding home, Grandmother
retold Hawthorne's story,
The Great Stone Face, and we searched
outcropping rocks of mountains
for a face we could grow to resemble.

HER WAY OF TALKING

Grandmother
was either
dressed fit to kill,
all tuckered out,
or *not worth shooting.*

One morning
she said she was
journey proud.
She opened
her trunk, put on
her hat, and
stood by the window
waiting.

THE FAVORITE

This morning moving close
the eyes ask first,
Who do you like best?
My son's small body shouting
me, choose me.

Long ago I asked my grandmother
as I sat in what was left
of her wide lap. I'd trace deep lines
down her cheeks, marvel how she
still could see through dusty glasses,
hear everything she shouldn't,
nothing she was supposed to.

I knew all seven children,
lived close with one, my mother,
and her, our matriarch,
her musty, drooping violets
pinned above a rhinestone button.

Which of her seven would she choose?
I watched them come, the sons,
six of them. I listened,
knew the child she lived with
never was the one.

Grandmother didn't say
no matter what she thought
inside her dark crepe dress, but
every time he left, her purse lay empty.
A distance settled on her,
and for a day or so
she never sang.

MOTHERS AND DAUGHTERS

Mother, as she studied me in church
stared at my nails, hands, the mole
and fine hair of my arms, at my chin
and nose, at the dress she made
that I was wearing, not exactly
of my choosing. There was nowhere
to go from her gaze.
This was her only chance
because hour by hour I was
pulling away. The door to my room
was closing.

        So I try not to
stare at my daughters, one by one
when they come near the soft lamp
of this household. The menu
is love, not scrutiny.
They have their own dishes
and double sinks. We look
from separate windows
into the world's street
and sometimes at table,
still forget the blessing.

MY HIDING TREE CUT FOR THE WOODPILE

burns blue.
Flame fire-wraps fir logs
as my sitting limb
axe-split
straddles andirons.

From this limb I watched
a long road
with no one coming
all the way to the curve.

SEEING

But I cannot observe
if you go too.
Distraction's child,
I will notice your hands,
warmth your arm against me brings,
that hollow your collar barely hides.

                    Evening comes,
and I must see the stars:
if they climb the far meadow's tree
the way they did last night
or different in another, darker sky.
With you, these eyes aren't mine.

THE UNDOING

If Natasha dies of cancer,
it will be because she loves
chocolate.
A reason good as any.
Not that eating darkness
harms you or me,
some serrated cunning skewers the matter
most at hand,
sight edging into night
when printed word and picture
are breath.

Those most dear undo us
yet days without dependency
lie valueless as zeroes
dead as the soft, headless mouse
a cat left by my door.

POCKETBOOKS

I was not born with one
except for that small crease

that helped them choose my name.
But they taught me to need one.
A sign in the library says
Keep your purse with you at all times.
Even in public bathrooms there's a hook for it.
How expected.

But mine holds in its dark corner
a seashell from wet sand, free feet
and wind that pulls to cold waves.
My fingers find one shiny franc
from near the Seine
where silent early men fish under bridges.

I remember coming home, how I threw down
that leather envelope molded to my body
with credit card and passport
tickets to temporary survival
glad to be rid of it sewn to my skin so long
it smelled of me.

Grandmother in the nursing home
carried hers so long
beaded black and worn
with twisted clasp I never could undo
she'd stir in her sleep
shiny transparent fingers
picking at the sheet picking
My bag, my bag, where is it?
Who's taken it? My bag.

from

Small Potatoes

Inside one potato there are mountains and rivers.
—Shinkichi Takahashi

BINOCULAR

From our window
on the marsh, look
how egrets roost
like white handkerchiefs
among high branches.
One flies,
a shape shifter
who lifts like laundry windblown
or prayer rising.

I USED TO LAUGH

At women in the beauty parlor
reading *Modern Screen* and *People*
heads tucked in oversized acorns
bodies bibbed
having work done on their nails,
their eyes, and feet.

It seemed a safe place for being ugly
a metamorphous hotel
where cocoons opened.
The transformed wrote checks,
swiped credit cards,
emerged into the world,
sprayed, perfumed,
colored, frosted,
purged of problems
left curled in the
hairdresser's ear.

THE RIDER

She pushes her bike up my hill and another,
down the road to the store, around by the church.
Miles she rides, up, level, and down.
Every day I pass her, pushing or riding
from out in the country past my house to town.
It is not an athletic thing she is doing.
The way she does it, the look in her eye.
Nor is it for food or a trinket she needs.

I am new to this road, this house, this view,
and I ask my neighbor, *Who is this woman?*
Not even he knows; but her primitive journey,
she rides out of something, a woman pursued.

She's a message in search of a mailbox
as she pedals my road moving
north, south, north all day.
And some nights without lights.
She rides. She pushes. She rides.

CEDARS

Dark flames
in a field at dusk,
these shaggy-barked cedars
are like favorable words.
Up the hillside
they straggle green,
random,
sown by birds.

AFTER THE STATION WAGON
AFTER THE VAN

This
little
car
I
love.

HIGHWAY

So close

was death

I felt

her cool breath slide by.

FAR FROM HOME

Sunday morning in another country
under the same sky,
the radio says the weather here
is weather there and although I have
work to do, I wander into town,
walking downhill a mile - a diner, coffee, paper,
and on my way uphill I see a church, a couple
entering in overcoats, elderly, holding hands
and the open door shows a sexton
at the end of his rope about to ring the bell
as I did once beneath my father's hairy hands.
I wander in and since it's Unitarian,
they're casual friendly, but do not pry or try me on
or sign me up or ask my story. Inside,
they're getting ready. The minister finds
his verses, someone lights candles,
and a man upfront in a Dr. Seuss hat, holds out a jar
of homemade pickles. He opens it and says,
They're Clara Thompson's. He tastes one – *mm* –
and offers one to a girl in the second row.
She likes it too. He says four jars by Clara will be
sold at Saturday's silent auction. *What time?*
he wonders and someone in the back says, *7:30.*
So we know absent Clara who may be our Holy Ghost,
our Mary, our priest, her pickles better
than a pallid wafer, that expected host. The minister
comes with poetry (Larkin and Sassoon) and comfort,
asks us to love one another, to give up being first.
After Chopin, Pucell, Tallis, the small choir sings.
Someone's child is crying. Going out, a woman
in silver beads, her velvet hat crushed sideways,
smiles welcome to this stranger on the way uphill,
(snow deeper now) sliding into drifts, praising
ritual in foreign lands, pickles on a Sunday.

UNDERNEATH

A hole is a serious thing
when a repairman's wheel goes
where there's nothing beneath,
and he walks from his truck, comes
to my door, his crew
standing around the long front yard,
hands in pockets, peaceful workmen waiting.
Ma'am, I think we're in your septic tank.
I say, *It's way out back.*
Well, he mutters, *a water line then to the road.*
I say, *No, we're not on city,*
we have a well, and he says, *Well,*
whatever it is we're in it.

FOOLISH UMBRELLA

I bought you at Bloomingdale's
that rainy day in the city,
stranded
at Lexington and 59th.
The saleswoman said
I needed the expensive one,
the sturdy umbrella, that you,
with your question marks on a field of orange,
would collapse in the hurling wind
and I saw what she meant that night
on theater streets littered
with forlorn wrecks of umbrellas
like broken wings.
You defied her. You lasted.

I carried you home
to Saturday markets
and movies, through all lonely weather,
but now, by mistake
I've left you for good
on a bus in Savannah
somewhere between General Sherman,
John Wesley,
and Juliette Gordon Low.
You will go on to umbrella adventures
and I, one less attachment
to things of this world.

Maybe one day I'll walk
shiny streets of Toronto
and see you bobbing
or beside a green
doorway in Charleston,
leaning.

SIGNS

Between Briar Creek
and a road called Runnymede,
the colors of air change.
It's an immanence I remember,

this moment of rainbow
backed up to darkness,
a moving mist with light
like a saint wears.
In search,
I speed unfamiliar streets
seeking a hill
to view what has to be.
The signs are right.

You know how it ends,
how rainbows aren't overtaken
like bandits on the road
but come soft,
silent, unaware,
a lucky time.

OLD ARGUMENT

In your staccato house,
you two
play an odd crescendo,
that fierce fight
which is your song.

AT FIFTY, WHAT IT COMES DOWN TO

Some people want fame
or lovers or gain,
but I would be wise and thin.
Yet if I were wise,
I would advise,
abandon thin and sin.

ORACLE/SCRIBE

Sorrow is the snake no one lets in.
He slides across shingles while we're out,
wraps the lamp base warmth,
and later like an oracle,
I watch in evening light.

He's mosaic in terrazzo,
bronze and golden walnut burl
on the table where I rattle words
like runes, casting them, line and curl.

Oracle, snake, quill, knife
and that culprit, life.

CANTICLE

Like a new candle
in an old cathedral,
hope wavers,
falters,
holds.

Songs On Silent Water

VOICES FROM THE PAST

SONGS ON SILENT WATER

John White, Approaching Roanoke Island, August 1590
His fifth voyage to Virginia

The winds are voices, Hasten, hasten.
I came as artist, governor, and now return,
a father searching shore imploring.
Three years held us in London, wars, and royal whim,
and now, sail this long, long journey once again.

To the island's end we glimpse a great fire
through woods, and in exceeding darkness, sail
for it like God's own beacon.
We row steadfast now, after England,
the Azores, past Hatteras with supplies
and succor and those dear letters.
As each oar pulls closer, darkness frames
imagined faces who waved goodbye - my daughter
Eleanor, and in her arms her daughter,
our colony's first child, today she will be three.
In air I draw each feature and fair tendril.

Soon we let fall the grapnel, quick
to catch the shore. We sound a trumpet call
and afterwards familiar English tunes,
our songs played to marsh grass, to ears we pray
are hearing, and we call to them friendly.

No answer. A continent of darkness, silent.
We lay within the boat throughout the night,
and all around us English tunes, lost
yet merry on the water.

At daybreak when we land, we find fire, grass
with rotten logs burning, and
through island woods, we cross and come to where
we left the village, that hungry life.

The sand lies trod by unshod feet
of savages, slim toes beside our boot prints.
As we mount the sandy bank, a tree,
carved with fair Roman letters – CRO –
a secret token when last we met, to leave
a sign on tree or doorpost if they depart.
A destination. As promised, we will follow.
Where houses were, deer eat melons.
O three years! And on another tree-post, tall
as a ship-boy's eye, CROATOAN. But no cross
carved, + that signal of distress we did agree on.
But on the sand, my books lie strewn,
torn from their covers.

Next morning we weigh anchor to Croatoan
to find our dear lost colony.
The wind is good for that near country.

But sudden weather grows from fair to foul.
West and northwest does the storm flail
so forcibly we bear no sail. Such blowing
would tear leaves and limbs from trees. It batters
us. Our fore-course half mast high, we turn
upon the wind perforce, and damaged by the storm
we make course, not Croatoan, nor Trinidad
for wintering and sweet return in spring.
Winds and Queen and Ship ever are our captains.
Blown to the North Atlantic, we limp
toward England, pray to stay afloat,
those urgent faces far behind us
like songs on silent water.

NIGHT WALKING

Dorothy Wordsworth and her brother William in Grasmere, England c 1800

In snow, rain or moon
at night I often walk alone to Ambleside to get the post
      –letters from William when he is gone
      –letters from Coleridge
      –letters bringing news but little else
We walk and sit upon a certain stone,
view Silver How, walk Langdale, each time new.
I need only William,
this moon upon the lake,
bare winter woods of stately shape and form,
gooseberries to feast upon,
the strange light upon White Moss,
bridges where we lean and look,
the becks – tumbling brooks – that language
of the countryside,
the sound of sheep, settled into sleep,
who sense my presence walking past, and shift
alarmed, then settle, reassured, as I pass on.

The lifting of the mists along the lake
is so alive it speaks my love for William.
Once, alone on an upland path, mists
blinded me. I sat, waited as the cloud whirled round.
When it moved, I overlooked a cliff.
One night, caught in a storm, I crawled on all fours
to find the way and later heard three men died
upon that pass, that winter month, lost
when their lantern sputtered out.

This walking nights is what life seeks, the cusp
of beauty that is danger.
William writes into his poems what I see,
and when I copy them, sends them to the world
who soon will come to him.

We know these paths.
When moonlight shows the way,
I gather moss. And in my garden, plant lemon thyme
beneath the moon, then go in to bed.

It is only ten o'clock.
At night upstairs and down, I walk.
In bed, I walk the ceiling.
Dear William has married.
He has brought Mary to our cottage.
The day before they wed, he gave me
the ring to hold for him. I wore it to bed
and gave it as he left for the village church.
I did not go. Wakeful, I go downstairs softly,
touch their door in passing,
run my fingers along the sturdy table
in the chilly parlour, stir the kitchen fire
banked for morning.

The early Grasmere village years of walking in all weather in the
English Lake District and living in Dove Cottage were among poet
William Wordsworth's most productive and Dorothy's happiest.
(Grasmere Journals 1800-03)

WIDOW
Susan Nye Hutchison, Charlotte, North Carolina

October 9, 1838
From Poughkeepsie to Raleigh
was not such a journey
as the four years since he died.
This living without him,
I must keep doing it.

With death at my back I stumble off the steamboat,
then the train with the children, and at last
the rickety stagecoach in dark, heavy rain.
Horses straining toward Salisbury,
the drunken driver swearing like Jehu, furious.
The carriage dips and leans in the limb-slapping night
careening. Hell must be like this.

October 15 I have come all this way for this.
With sad heart I commence to teach ten or twelve scholars.

October 29 Six more pupils. I should have sixty.
Where are the children? Churning butter, spinning cotton,
running in cemeteries, everywhere but here in my class.
I could harvest their minds like flowers,
those bright eyes.

May 20, 1839 A great luxury. After school
I took a warm bath at Mrs. Fisher's.

October 19, 1839
Arrived in Charlotte to open a school
for young ladies. We begin tomorrow.
Neighbors sent vegetables, honey.
General muster here, so no school today.
Here come the people – families in wagons.
Picnic baskets. Men with their muskets
in from the farms parade the streets, rag-taggle army.
What do they fear?

April 19, 1840   At church my son Adam
sits in the Baptist balcony
with the colored people. One small white mask
in a dark covey of faces. He likes looking down on us —
men on one side, women on the other.
Fidgety children scattered by sex among them.
Town ladies send carriages to take us riding.

May 1   Big celebration.
The graveyard so beautiful
shady oaks overlaying the churchyard.
Were it not for this square despair would claim me.
I learn the names on tombstones,
Polk, Graham, Mason, McComb, McKnight, how they
came by wagon, by horseback,
when there was even less than this.
All these monuments. So much rubbish tossed round.

May 3   Great opposition in town
to my teaching math to young ladies.

May 23   Sabbath. We ride to the river, cross it
then late in the day set out for home.
Water rising over our wagon wheels higher
than morning's rushing mud level. Oh, we are fearful!
Captain Neel's son leads us on his horse, sure-footed
in shallows, then deep as my son's shoulder,
the stone-bottomed way of the ford. We weave
back across the brown-pocked Catawba
sluggish then swirling. Not for a long while
will I venture another river.

August 30   At Sugar Creek in the open air
a vast crowd at preaching.
Eighty minutes of Dr. Leland are too many.

The money I've made barely settles my debts.
I began here owing, came with only
clothes on our bodies, my books.
Now after a year supporting my children,
I have a house. Humble furniture.

November 12 ...I am kept awake by rejoicing.
Men's voices. Whoop and hoorah. The sound
of one man's voice still never far
from me after almost six years. I wake
thinking he will come through my door,
take off his shoes, first his left,
then his right.

Who wants to know
how it is for a woman alone?
Surely someone will ask.

HOW LIFE WAS

Harriet Jacobs, a mulatto slave born 1813 in Edenton, North Carolina

In my slant corner beneath the roof
there is so little space I can't
extend my feet even when I sleep.
If I survive, I'll be crippled as a broken stick.
Anything's better than how life was.

From little crooked holes along the eaves
I watch my enemy, the doctor,
go past. He owns me,
but not my children who are free as redbirds.
I see them play beneath the trees.
They do not know I watch.

One day the doctor offers them
gay handkerchiefs and shiny silver coins
to tell him where I am.
Gone North, I hear them say. Next day
a dog attacks my son, chews him bloody.
I hear his screams as they sew his wounds.
Next day he's out again and playing.
My children's freedom! Oh,
anything's better than how life was.

Only Grandmother and Uncle Phillip know
my hiding place. Between the eaves
Uncle built this box I lie in.
Each day I hear street talk below me –
yesterday slave hunters planning how
to catch some poor fugitive. Sometimes I hear
the doctor's gone North again to find me.

Rain trickles through my roof.
Scorching heat and insects. Frostbite.
I dare not cough or sneeze or light a candle.
Each day the man whose slave I am
passes down King Street to his office.
He has dark uses for me.

Seven years in this dismal hole
before we find a way to flee.
But anything's better than how life was.

TO MAKE HER LOVE ME

Henry Bibb in 1849 was a slave before escaping north.

Take this one particular
bone out of a bullfrog and dry it. Then
when I approach the girl I choose,
scratch her naked skin
with that frog bone, she will love me.
That's no easier than smoothing
a live red fox at nightfall.
The girl I want is Lucy, I see her
walking out with Sam on Sunday evenings.
It takes some doing to get close.
I scratch her neck.
She likes to kill me.

So I try Phoebe.
I pay a conjur man,
he says I need a lock of the girl's hair, put it
in my shoe and I will have her.
I ask her nice. She jerks away.
I don't let go. She screech and I
pull a patch of hair, but that's all
I get from Phoebe.

Last week I pay old conjur Henry, ask him
make my master not to whip me.
He say chew a bitter root, go to the cow pen
at night, take fresh manure, mix it
with red pepper and a white man's hair,
put it in a pot and stir, scorch it,
grind it fine like snuff, scatter
a pinch in master's room at night
when I lay his fire, some in the corner,
a bit on his linen, so when he breathes it,
old Henry say, my master will not flog me.
I did it all.
I stayed away that night without permission.
Next morning I talk saucy to my master.
I'm like a teasing mouse standing by a hole.
In spite of all my roots and powders,
he whips me.

CORNFIELD
Mariah, a slave, 1850

That day I hoed the back field,
watching the old rhythm of woods,
chant and chop
pull and step sideways
reach chop pull
again again,
heat under my head rag, me
thinking only reach chop pull, thinking
of Elias in Africa, when past my head
goes something dark. A shape
lands ten rows away,
a bird like indigo, huge
that stares,
then waits, then moves.
Strange. Bigger
than crow, buzzard maybe,
or great dark duck,
it stayed and watched, then flew.
And when the drums said
Elias died in Africa at corn time,
I knew.

WALKING THE YORKSHIRE MOORS WITH CHARLOTTE BRONTE

Elizabeth Gaskell, Bronte's biographer, returns to Haworth, England 1856

I.

Until I came to Haworth, how could I know
the woman, the fire that burned
as if some spirit lamp in her were kindled.
I never saw its like elsewhere.

Until I came, I could not see her mockery
of Austen's confined fences, bordered gardens,
fragile flowers, and ladies. For Austen – no glimpse
of wild, open country. No far hill.

Until I came to Haworth, I did not hear
its silence nor the wind, the howl, her high house
stranded above a stark village of gray stone,
its street so steep, horses slid.

Until I saw, I did not feel how desolate
a place can be. Hungry, treeless fields.
Long, leaden hills bleak in all directions.
No wonder pupils never came.

She knew each rock, each cottager for miles
and they knew her. I learned her confines – not fence
and moor, but Father. Sisters. Brother. Churchyard
of mossy graves waiting out her window.

Until I came, I did not see how strangers
made her ill, how small she was, how she
could not converse if her rocker sat askew,
nor could I tell, until I knew.

II.

As Charlotte and I walked
beyond her village onto the moors' vast beauty,
a woman loaned her an umbrella.
In another isolated house, we took shelter.
At three miles from home, a chair was dusted for her,
    Sit ye down, Miss Bronte.
We parted, and agreed, since I live in Manchester,
if she wanted bustle, or if I wanted quiet,
we were to let each other know.

III.
Here's how it was:

Papa, I have been writing a book.
        Have you, my dear, and he went on reading.
But Papa, would you look at it?
        I can't be troubled with a manuscript.
Papa, I have had it printed.
        I hope you didn't make silly expense.
May I read you some reviews?
He nodded.
I did, then asked, Would you read my book?
        Leave it. And I will see.

That afternoon he called us in to tea and said,
Children, Charlotte has been writing a book.
It is better than I expected.

He did not mention JANE EYRE *again until much later.*
We dare not tell him of the books my sisters write.

IV
After Charlotte died in '55, her father Patrick,
who outlived first his wife, then all six children,
wrote asking me to write a book
about her life.
I am a novelist – not a biographer – but I went
to that wayward, silent, Irish father
who had shot pistols out the upstairs parsonage window
when he was angry, or once, in a rage
sawed legs from the household chairs.

But when he asked, I did.

Elizabeth Gaskell's THE LIFE OF CHARLOTTE BRONTE *was published in London in 1857. Gaskell, well known for her popular novels, some serialized in Charles Dickens' magazine,* THE CORNHILL, *is honored in Poet's Corner of London's Westminster Abbey.*

DIRT

Mary Boykin Chesnut of South Carolina, February, 1865,
Lincolnton, North Carolina.

I forgot my English tea
on the mantelpiece
in Columbia. I was the last
refugee. Now exiled, safe
we have come
to this most out of the way
of all places, off all Yankee routes,
Sherman rising to Columbia toward Camden,
and we, chased from town, from our plantation.
He left a trail black as prairie fire.

My trunks of clothes
stayed in Richmond, and everything else
in Columbia, even the negroes
except for my maid Ellen
and Laurence, our man.
Here in a room at Mrs. McLean's
I stir the wood fire, grateful.
To stay four days, we pay $240,
an ungodly sum, still she is a lady,
a lily in a dark bed.

Dirt everywhere!
A soldier on the train from Charlotte
offered two biscuits
wrapped in a filthy rag.
Ellen scrubs windows, floors,
tobacco juice from the wall.
I polish brass and irons, so pretty.
Much is amiss here, but
they can bake bread;
few women of beauty
and refinement come to call.
Our Confederate money
buys nothing – not even onions.

With Mr. Chesnut in Charlotte –
this dirt is safer.
As in Dr. Palmer's last sermon,
We are on a lone rock –
the waters closing.

Someone rushes to say
Sherman left Columbia
in ashes, close behind me.
Charleston and Wilmington surrendered.
I shall read no more papers.
Nothing left in his tracks,
only lone chimneys
standing like telegraph poles
to carry dire news.

BODIES

When I think of bodies piled in trenches,
the sharp stink of summer death
and winter's fixed posture of frozen bodies, arms
everywhere and frozen feet,
it is Baba Yar and Auschwitz.

But no, up my southern road
a long, soft mound of dirt slowly settled
into that gradual grass of forgetting
a mass grave of 5,000 maybe more.
Again in my life, I am wrong. I am wrong,
somewhere nothing is forgotten.
In a historic Salisbury house fifty miles
north, close by the rail line, here is the sketch
of the town's tall brick cotton mill
used for a Civil War prison.
At first, prisoners mingled
in the village and traded for tobacco.
But the war that was not supposed to last
slogged on. As wars do.
Prisoners were no longer exchanged
for the enemy's, and no one left except in death
and not even then.

Behind the stockade, the stench of filth
and torment of rats at night,
the acrid smoke and years of awful crowding –
10,000 men moved through here
in space for 1,000 in a town not much bigger,
both men and townspeople at night
awake and listening.

As I walk the streets of the quiet town
what's wrong is to forget those nights
and that day captives were freed –
men who ate corn cob pudding
and mouse soup – trudging north to freedom,
anyone who could, in a line two miles long, wearing
the coarse clothes of the dead.

THE ONLY THING I FEAR IS A COW AND A DRUNKEN MAN

*Elizabeth Allston Pringle, a wellborn but landless widow, bought back two
of her family's rice plantations, lost to creditors following the Civil War.*

So graceful are the women as they sow
rice with waving motions, arch
bending low to keep wind from scattering grain,
their skirts tied round their hips,
their swinging walk. Beneath their skirts
two narrow sacks hold my seed rice
saved for planting.
If weighed before they leave the field,
the women would be found to gain many pounds
were I to turn my back as they dip rice after planting.
But their tender sympathy is more to me
than many bushels

I have a thousand acres
but not a cent of money.
I'm puzzled beyond all measure
what to do next year. Impossible
to go on planting rice if it's to sell
at forty cents a bushel. How will I pay
the mortgage? $1000 this year. Will the bank renew?
And then the taxes.

As far as my seed rice will go,
I will rent land to the negroes for shares,
for all of us, rice is our life,
our food, our work, our spectacle.

But Mr. Z, the first white help I've had,
set bonfires near my threshing mill and barns.
Wild flames roaring to the moon. I shoveled
dirt onto his fires, and caught murder in his eye,
as whenever he gets to drinking.

December 31 1905
At year's end I wonder if
God wills I give it up, this planting rice,
this life of isolation, my simple
living close-heart to the land.
Beauty is a life itself.
But with the sluice gates and field banks storm-broken
and no means to repair them,
all this fine land without skilled hands to work it,
what good is knowing from my father
this intricate routine of rice, the tides and tending,
the time of ricebirds' ravenous migrations.
I look on the broad expanse
to bottom land where cotton did not prove success.
I stand toward the river's marsh-edged soil,
remember the early green of rice, which turned
hues of golden sheen
ever moving as water.

I must not be too stubborn
to see His message.

*Pringle described her exuberant and difficult life as a coastal South Carolina
planter and as overseer of black laborers and sharecroppers, also many of
her father's former slaves or their descendants. But the great storm in 1906 and
subsequent bad weather ruined coastal rice banks and floodgates. Carolina rice
plantations became hunting preserves, private winter retreats, and vast timberlands.*

AT THE MERCURY MILL
Helen, 1920s, North Carolina

Our three room house
belonged to the mill.
We filled it.
Mother. Four children.
Father had gone.
Mother worked the spinning room
at the front of the mill.
We stayed by ourselves, but
felt her watching
from the mill window.

We knew not to cross
those railroad tracks or
climb the water tank. She
showed us how to do.
Her boss let her come
at nine and noon and three
long enough to nurse the baby.
For $2.20 a day
her shift was eleven hours.
Nights she cooked and washed
and ironed. Then
she got sick.

I was twelve
two years too young by law
to work, but the doctor
changed my age on the paper
and I swept floors
at the mill,
piles of lint, until
they found out, until
she got well.
I remember that mill.

BY MYSELF
Sculptor Anna Hyatt Huntington, Paris Salon of 1910 to Brookgreen

By myself, I built that life-size horse
with Joan astride, tall in armor,
sword held high for God to bless at Orleans.
The French said I could not have
done it alone, a woman sculpting large.
So they withheld a medal.

I studied skeletons. In my brother's field
I watched how horses' muscles stretch
and leg bones settle shifting weight.
I took my small, damp piece of clay
to model with my fingers what I saw.
In my studio I made it large.

At the Balchalx Circus during training times
in France, I took clay to capture horses, lions,
all in motion. I studied at the pungent stables
of Magasin des Beaux Arts, a store
with delivery horses trotting up and down.
To my walk-in studio they sent a handsome bay.
I knew those horses, felt them
without touching, watching muscles.

In the Bronx Zoo early mornings, before
they tossed raw meat to the jaguar, I watched
to hear the trainer shout, and at that shout,
the jaguar paused an instant on her limb,
then plunged to feed.
That moment, one glimpse each morning.

In New York, I was a woman in my 40s,
sculpting cranes, lions, greyhounds,
my *Diana of the Chase*,
making art, making money, 1920s when
a large man brought a sculpture commission.

I did marry him, although I hadn't planned to —
that tall American, Archer, a Spanish scholar
who loved sculpture, Spain, and horses.
Because of him, my *Rosinante*
of *Don Quixote*. My equestrian *El Cid*.
I didn't tell my family how rich he was.
Life was my gift to him. His to me,
ever freedom.

We bought four low-country rice plantations,
side by Carolina side, thousands of acres,
where gray tendrils of Spanish moss swayed
in coastal breeze along the grand avenue of oaks
and an abandoned boxwood garden.
If ever there arose from earth an air of beauty,
I found it there.

Among the dunes we built our winter home,
its tall, brick Moorish tower — an atalaya-
like those that guard the Spanish coast,
an austere walled courtyard, sand colored
with a high-roofed studio for me
to sculpt my horses.

At 90, despite aching hands and knees,
I sculpted Andrew Jackson,
but I made him the Carolina farm boy he was,
barefoot in rustic clothes, sitting sideways
bare back, of course
one hand behind him on his horse's rump,
gazing onto fields as I did long ago
in my brother's pasture, sitting in meadow grass
watching horses.

Both the Huntingtons' Moorish beach home Atalaya (1931) and adjacent marshside Brookgreen Gardens with about 600 sculptures, are on the National Register of Historic Places. Both extend the Huntingtons' stunning vision of a serene public sculpture garden and nature and wildlife preserve on former rice plantations. For this, Archer Milton Huntington (1870-1955) acquired about 10,000 acres in parcels in the 1930s. Anna (1876-1973) is widely celebrated for her powerful animal and equestrian sculptures, such as Jaguar Reaching *and* Fighting Stallions *at Brookgreen, and work in over 200 American museums, Canada and Spain. She donated her evocative equestrian sculpture of young Jackson to the children of South Carolina for the Andrew Jackson State Park. The beachside property containing Atalaya is the Huntington Beach State Park in South Carolina near Pawley's Island.*

RUE DE FLEURUS, GERTRUDE WALKING
Gertrude Stein in Paris 1910

Walking from *Rue de Fleurus* step by step
across Paris, across the Seine
finally uphill to Montmartre,
I wear language of eyes, swallow sounds
of streets, alive, alone in English,
scrape and sand the words within
until I come to the door
of the wooden building on *Rue Ravignan*.
Dog smell in there and Picasso lets me in,
his wonderful eyes. Behind and around him
enormous pictures. I sit in the armchair
for long, still hours. He paints as I pose,
just sit, lean forward.
I don't recall how this happened,
although little is without choosing.
Who remembers how he asked,
how I agreed? It's not important.
We talk some as he dabs his palette brown
and it goes, the time. Phrases within me
revolve. I take them apart and rearrange.

Ninety times in all, I go
or was it eighty? He's Picasso, young, poor
and on Saturdays when he's done,
he and Fernande walk home with me
the long dark walk across Paris.
Dinner waits and we sit with the walls
of pictures: Braque, Cezanne, Matisse, Renoir
and Picasso's we bought from him
so he could pay the grocer. While walking
beautiful Fernande talks hats, perfume, furs.
Picasso and I argue. We understand
each other. Art and sentences.

Tuesday I walk again across the city
carrying for him in my overcoat pocket
American comics. At each corner,
each café I pass, coming back, coming down,
scenes of the street weave my sentences,
the fugue of feet saying, saying
what is and is not how.

One day in spring, he painted out my head,
painted it blank in the portrait,
and when he came back from Spain in winter
while I was gone, he finished it.
He was content. So was I.
It's all there, he said, even though
over summer I'd cut away my hair.

While in Paris, Gertrude Stein wrote THREE LIVES *and*
THE MAKING OF AMERICANS.

VIRGINIA WOOLF AND OCTAVIA

Physician and friend, Dr. Octavia Wilburforce, comes to tea often during the English winter of 1941.

Please come, Leonard said.
Of course, I did.

Winter and war and her novel's end lay across her.
Her work ripe and abundant like the grapes of Nineveh.

I think of it now when I cross the Ouse,
the slow calm strand that could be any river.

When I pour cream and spread Guernsey butter
on thick bread, I see her slim hand pour tea.

When I take down my walking stick and go past Rodmell,
the river has found its old path.

The winter I went for tea she showed me the new river
the bombing brought – old banks burst upstream –

what had been far and thin came toward us wide.
The meadow floated, green-oval islands.

She said she would write my portrait.
Whatever for, I smiled, but I went often

for I too loved her.
She was a thin river beyond its bounds.

And when Leonard called, I came. I undressed her,
pale and angular, with icy hands. She feared

the dark and leaving. I gave words and cream.
What she needed, no physician owns.

My walking stick is oak, my father's.
And when I walk south, I see

Leonard run that last day to her stick
left in the riverbank far upstream.

Did my coming – as doctor,
not friend – undo her?

Had I known more,
would she have lingered?

She was no more mad than I.
I am the one with dreams – a walking stick and cream,

her thin hand, and those fluid,
green-oval, meadow islands.

Mary Kratt, a native of West Virginia, has lived most of her life in Charlotte, North Carolina. Her poems have appeared in numerous literary magazines and anthologies. She is a winner of the Brockman-Campbell Poetry Book Award, Oscar Arnold Young Poetry Book Award, Peace History Book Prize, St. Andrews Writer in Community Award, and the Irene Blair Honeycutt Legacy Award. Her nonfiction books feature the Piedmont region of the Carolinas. She taught English and American Studies at UNC-Charlotte and currently lives in Charlotte with her husband Jim.